To See
His Face

... to feel His Touch
... to hear His Voice

Dearest Mia —
you are HIS
Beloved!
May you see His face
more clearly, feel His touch
more gently, and hear His
Voice more distinctly
each & every moment of
each day.
With love —
faith

Book One in
"Your Royal Heritage" series

FAITH GALLATIN

Verses marked NASB are taken from the NEW AMERICAN STANDARD BIBLE®,
Copyright © 1960,1962,1963,1968,1971,1972, 1973,1975,1977,1995
by The Lockman Foundation. Used by permission.

Verses marked NIV are taken from the HOLY BIBLE, NEW INTERNATIONAL
VERSION®. Copyright © 1973, 1978, 1984 International Bible Society.
Used by permission of Zondervan. All rights reserved.
The "NIV" and "New International Version" trademarks are registered in the
United States Patent and Trademark Office by International Bible Society. Use of
either trademark requires the permission of International Bible Society.

Verses marked NKJV are taken from the New King James Version.
Copyright © 1982 by Thomas Nelson, Inc. Used by permission. All rights reserved.

Verses marked "The Message" are taken from *The Message*.
Copyright © 1993, 1994, 1995, 1996, 2000, 2001, 2002.
Used by permission of NavPress Publishing Group.

Verses marked KJV are taken from the King James Version, Public Domain.

ISBN-10: 1448645549
ISBN-13: 9781448645541

This book is for
all my New Song sisters — you know who you are,
my blood sisters, Ruth and Kathleen,
and my heavenly cheerleaders, Lori, Diana, and Rachel.
I love you all so much!

I Chronicles 16:8-11 KJV
Give thanks unto the LORD, call upon his name,
make known his deeds among the people.
Sing unto him, sing psalms unto him,
talk ye of all his wondrous works.
Glory ye in his holy name:
let the heart of them rejoice that seek the LORD.
Seek the LORD and his strength,
seek his face continually.

Table of Contents

As You Embark

In May of 2004, I was given an assignment. It shouldn't have been a big deal at all to me. After all, I graduated with honors all through high school and college.

But this was different.

There was no right or wrong answer. I was supposed to explain, in any way I chose, what God had taught me over the past ten months.

Other ladies in my group were creating works of art, crafts extraordinaire, or amazing flower arrangements. I felt inadequate, unable to come up with even one interesting idea — let alone being able to summarize the past year in my spiritual life.

And then it was Thursday — the day the assignment was due.

I sat down at my computer and began to write about a house — because construction has been my profession for many years, and a house *is* a great analogy for many aspects of life.

I didn't know what I was going to say. But suddenly words flowed through my fingers. I printed it out and breathed a huge sigh of relief after reading it that night. It was finished.

Little did I know it was actually just the beginning.

Every year since then, I have been challenged with the same

assignment. And I have sat at my computer and typed.

And then I didn't need an assignment from a person to write. And it wasn't just once a year.

My assignments came from God as He spoke into my life — and they came much more frequently than I often wanted.

I shared what I wrote in my ladies' group. They said they saw His face. They said I wrote their exact thoughts. They began to ask — and then demand — when they could have a copy of my stories to read whenever they wished ... or needed.

So here they are. Stories pulled from the emotion-filled everyday life of a sister — so familiar to you, and yet open for your own details.

Please make them your own. Use the reflection questions in the back if you wish.

Allow Him to show you His face ... as you have never seen it before.

He will, you know ....

1
His Invitation

Best friends since kindergarten. Inseparable. If one was there, the other three weren't far away. Happy little girls skipping across playgrounds ... pretending to be mommies, super-heroines, and pirates ... laughing all the time. Giggling teenagers anxious to be noticed by a boy ... feeling ugly. Enchanting young women ... still friends, still engaged in life.

Personal letters were delivered by courier to each of the four girls one spring day. In loving tones, the letters said they were chosen by the High King to be adopted into his family as daughters. All they needed to do was accept his invitation and make their way to his castle to live with him forever.

All four girls were astonished ... then delighted ... then ecstatic about being chosen for this honor. The best part, however, was that they would all be together as sisters. They began to talk of what awaited them, how the king would treat them, what their lives would be like in his castle.

But you know how life is.

The girls kept busy with graduation plans, life plans, family plans ... and they gradually grew apart from each other. Life paths separated as each pursued her goals. Promises of friendship and sisterhood faded into yellowed photographs.

Years passed. Addresses and phone numbers changed. Communication ceased.

One lazy summer day, four women collided at the entrance to a local coffee shop. Their faces turned quickly to those next to them. It was a familiar face — all of them were. Excited cries rose to the lips of the four women. The friends were all there, once again together!

The four dove into the coffee shop, ordered lattes, and sat down to catch up. It had been far too long ... even though each secretly knew she could have stayed in touch if she had tried. But each had been afraid of responses from the others.

Masque was first to share. Her life in the city was so busy. Lively tales of friends, parties, events, and plans filled her dialogue. She was pursuing a career and going to the top. Her name was well known to many, giving her influence and power.

As she talked on, laughing often and gesturing wildly, the other three noticed a haunting sadness in her eyes. No matter what her mouth said, her eyes spoke a different tale. She admitted she still had the letter from the High King, but had been much too busy with her social acquaintances to contemplate — let alone pursue — his invitation. She never mentioned it to anyone any more.

Not-Good-Enough spoke up saying she was living together with a group of men and women who had all received invitations from the king. They had met on the way to his castle and decided to stop in the forest inside the castle grounds. Surviving on game and what they grew in their gardens, they were reasonably happy, living as a family, sharing the load of life's needs, encouraging one another through the endless problems of life.

Works smiled tiredly. Her voice was quiet. She had gone to the king's castle soon after graduation. As she approached by the front drive, a uniformed guard told her she must go in the rear door. She followed his directions and found herself welcomed by the kitchen servants and quickly trained in her duties. Works was thrilled to have a place where she could serve the king. Maybe she didn't serve him face to face, but she knew — and was reassured constantly by her colleagues — that he appreciated how she washed the dishes and scrubbed the kitchen floors every day. Her voice dropped off. She sat in silence for a few moments.

"Isn't there more to life than this?" she burst out. "Never ending sameness — always tired, always doing, never being truly joyful or fulfilled? I remember when we all dreamed of how amazing it would be to be the king's daughters. What happened to those dreams? Where did we go wrong?"

"You didn't believe him. You didn't accept his invitation at face value."

The fourth woman spoke. She had sat quietly while all the others shared their lives. The other three now turned to look at her.

"How do you know?" Masque queried.

"Because I did believe him and his invitation as true and

real. I walked right past that guard in the front drive. I even pushed my way past the butler at the front door. I clutched my invitation and searched the castle to find the High King. I had to know for sure he wanted me as his letter said.

"I'll never forget the moment he saw me. He turned away from everyone else in the room and ran to pull me into his strong arms and hug me tighter than I've ever been held before. He whispered how much he loved me and how happy he was that I was there — and that he never wanted me to leave again.

"Right then I knew he was for real. His words are true.

"I am his daughter in every sense of the word. I live in his castle with my own suite of rooms. I am provided with everything I need — and a fair amount of what I want. My daddy loves me and I love him. I spend time with him — just him and me — every day for as long as I want. He has given me opportunities to learn and develop all kinds of talents. He encourages me to be active using these abilities. Sometimes I pinch myself to see if it's all real, and it is. It's all he promised to us so long ago."

Daughter's eyes were shining as she spoke. Her body was relaxed and at peace. The other three were magnetically drawn to what she said. They wished ….

Daughter suddenly sprang from her seat. A handsome gentleman with touches of gray at his temples stepped through the door. She rushed into his arms.

"You're here!" she cried. "I had no idea you were coming to

town today! Please come and meet my childhood friends whom I haven't seen in years. We were just catching up."

She dragged him over to their table. The other three girls jumped to their feet and curtsied.

The High King reached out and lifted Masque's face so her eyes met his.

"Hello, my darling Masque!" His voice was deep and oh so comforting. "I've missed you at my castle. Been really busy, haven't you? Well, I'm waiting for when you have a moment in your calendar to meet with me." He smiled gently.

"Not-Good-Enough, my dearest. I love you … do you know that? I want you to have dinner with me — not once, but every night. Bring all your friends with you, too. I want them all *inside* my castle; the forest is too far away for me!" His gaze held hers steadily, lovingly.

"Works, my sweetheart. You are much too tired. I want you upstairs, next to Daughter, taking a long, well-earned rest. I've waited for you to come upstairs. Can you do that for me?" His eyes encouraged her with depths of unspoken tenderness.

He sighed.

"Darling Daughter, I must get back to the castle. Do you want to ride with me?"

Daughter smiled. "No thanks, Daddy. I need a few more moments with these sisters of mine."

The High King hugged her. He gently reached out to touch

the heads of the other three, as if in blessing. He turned and exited with a lingering backward glance at his daughters.

"Please think about what he said, girls," Daughter broke the magical silence. "I have missed you all so much. Wished every day you would suddenly show up at the castle and move in and be with me as my sisters — just as we always dreamed.

"It's *not* a dream. It is a reality if you will believe and receive his invitation. I know it still stands. Didn't you see it in his eyes? So will you?"

Jeremiah 31:3-4 NASB

The LORD appeared to him from afar, saying, "I have loved you with an everlasting love; therefore I have drawn you with lovingkindness. Again I will build you and you will be rebuilt, O virgin of Israel! Again you will take up your tambourines, and go forth to the dances of the merrymakers."

1 John 3:1-2 NIV

How great is the love the Father has lavished on us, that we should be called children of God! And that is what we are! The reason the world does not know us is that it did not know him. Dear friends, now we are children of God, and what we will be has not yet been made known. But we know that when he appears, we shall be like him, for we shall see him as he is.

Galatians 4:6-7 The Message

You can tell for sure that you are now fully adopted as his own children because God sent the Spirit of his Son into our lives crying out, "Papa! Father!" Doesn't that privilege of intimate conversation with God make it plain that you are not a slave, but a child? And if you are a child, you're also an heir, with complete access to the inheritance.

For reflection, see page 94.

To See His Face

II
His House —
The Burning

Screaming sirens pierced my eardrums. Acrid smoke seared the back of my throat. Hot tears stung my eyes and made rivulets of mud down my ash-covered cheeks.

I stared in disbelief at the remnants of my home ... my beautiful home that all my friends and neighbors envied and repeatedly told me so. The home I had built with my own hands, so carefully, so lovingly, so full of pride. All gone in a matter of minutes!

Thankful it was the middle of the night so no one could see my real pain and agony, I sat on the edge of the sidewalk as my shaking knees gave out. I watched the final two pieces of standing wall soaking up huge quantities of water from the fire hoses.

What was I to do now?

Then I saw him walking slowly toward me. It was my father. His stern expression was carved on his face, no smile or frown, not a flicker of emotion visible. I wanted to run and hide. You see, my father had financed the cost of the building which was now burnt ashes. I had never repaid him a penny because he said I didn't have to.

What would he say when he found out the cause of the fire? But, I could tell he had already spoken to the Battalion Chief.

I love burning candles everywhere to cast beautiful fragrances around my home. I had carelessly left one burning in the lower bathroom when I went to bed; somehow the flames escaped their holder and found much more to consume. It was directly my fault my home was gone — and my father's investment in shambles.

My father kept coming nearer and nearer. I tried pretending not to notice his approach, but inadvertently caught his eye with a quick glance to check his progress.

I began to weep. His eyes brimmed with love and concern. His step quickened and he pulled me up into his strong arms, squeezing me in a huge bear hug.

"My darling Baby Girl," he murmured in my ear as he rocked me gently. "You're alive! You're unhurt! That's all I hoped for!"

Sobs racked my body at his words. I could barely speak. "Daddy … I'm sorry! I didn't … mean to … burn it all up!" The words escaped me between huge gasps.

"Oh my child, don't worry about the house. It can be rebuilt. It's you I care about. You are important to me, no matter what you have done. I love you!"

"Aren't you mad at me? That's all your money gone," I cried.

"No, Baby Doll. Material things don't matter. I can tell you are truly sorry. I forgive you. I'm just so glad I still have you here to hold and comfort!"

He held me close for a long while, ignoring flashing lights and engine noises. I was safe in my daddy's arms, secure from anything trying to rob me from him. I knew beyond a shadow of a doubt he would protect me at all costs.

The next morning, Daddy and I shared breakfast in his warm kitchen. As we finished our coffee, he produced a set of blueprints he said he'd been saving in case I might ever be interested in building again. He said I could choose whether I wanted to use them or not, but he had them drawn up years before just for me.

I was awestruck at the amazing design on the pages before me. Every detail of this home felt right! Daddy had incorporated things I had never even thought of … and they *were* perfect for me.

I looked into his eyes. "But, Daddy, I have no money to build this house. I love these plans, but how can I ever use them now? I let the insurance policy lapse on my home, so I have nothing to even start with!"

"Baby Girl, I'll make a deal with you. I'll foot the bill again if you let me work with you on the rebuilding process. *And* if you will *listen* to my ideas as we go along. You don't have to accept them, but I want you to listen and consider them."

19

I stared at him for a moment. "You trust me to build again? Another house? At your cost?" I paused. I wasn't going to get a better deal than this anywhere else ... especially looking at the design in front of me.

"You've got yourself a deal," I smiled.

We've broken ground on my new home. As I promised Daddy, he is a part of every step along the way. We have a few disagreements; he is always patient with me as I vehemently express my opinions to him. He listens tenderly to my thoughts and shares his reasons behind his opinions so I find myself, once again, seeing my house as he designed it to be when it is finished.

This house is amazing beyond words — and it's not even half done yet! The plans showed none of the tiny details Daddy plans — none of the extra reinforced concrete or specialty cove molding trim; none of the top-end roofing or clear cedar gable shingles cut in a unique pattern; none of the imported stone for the huge back patio and planter walls.

My new home has a long way to go until it is finished, but it is already twice — no, way more than that — what my old house was. And it's because of my Daddy who is truly the best designer in the whole world. It's because he knows me inside and out — better than I know myself. And because *he's* the one in charge of the building process this time around.

Hebrews 3:4 NASB

For every house is built by someone, but the builder of all things is God.

Luke 6:48 KJV

He is like a man which built an house, and digged deep, and laid the foundation on a rock: and when the flood arose, the stream beat vehemently upon that house, and could not shake it: for it was founded upon a rock.

For reflection, see page 96.

To See His Face

22

III
His Forgiveness

Rough, wrenching hands. Elbows in my ribs. Fingers poking my back. My feet keep leaving the ground as I am pushed and pulled by men on all sides of me.

"This is a nightmare! " my mind keeps saying. "I'll wake up soon and it'll all be normal."

But pains in my body contradict my thoughts. The bruises I will have tomorrow ...!

Doors are flung open. Where on earth are they taking me?

My pounding heart stops dead in my chest. I am in the foyer of his house!

"No!" I hiss.

"Oh, yes, woman," gloats one man. "Now everyone will know what you really are!"

My body feels cold. I seem to see everything from a distance.

I am dragged through the hallway ... into His innermost sanctuary.

Thrown to the floor, I curl into a ball. Realization washes over me. They want *Him*! I am simply a pawn in a game of universal power. I am nothing ... completely insignificant ... just bait in this deadly struggle for control of souls. And I played into their trap. I who should have known better!

I cannot move. I daren't meet his eyes. Shame permeates my entire being. How could I have gotten myself into this position? Everyone else said it was just a "white lie," a "small deception," a "saving of another's feelings." But my heart speaks the truth now. It was sin – not completely doing the right thing which I knew to do.

Strong voices argue around me. My mind doesn't comprehend what is being said. I know what's coming — and I know I deserve it. Separation from my father, never again able to look at his face or feel his touch. Condemned forever to a place of heartbreak and aloneness.

Suddenly silence deafens the room. Footsteps slink away. The heavy breathing of predators disappears.

A touch on my chin. The gentlest of hands lifts my head. Tears course down my cheeks from my closed eyes. I'm trembling from head to toe.

"My darling daughter, open your eyes. Look at me."

I silently obey. His eyes are full of tears also, and amazing, intense love.

"Where are your accusers?"

I don't need to look. I know they are gone. Yes, they are *all* gone. *He* was never one of them.

"I am so sorry!" I blurt out, not having adequate words to express my heart of grief.

"I am, too. And that is why I died for you, my child," He breathes. "You are forgiven. Healed. Restored. Go, live, and with My strength, sin no more."

Washed clean. Forgiven and forgotten. A clean slate. A brand new day. A fresh, perfect beginning. It is truly a miracle.

Nothing I deserve … yet I receive it, embrace it, and will journey forward with His courage and grace.

And I am truly grateful.

John 8:10-12 KJV

When Jesus had lifted up himself, and saw none but the woman, he said unto her, "Woman, where are those thine accusers? hath no man condemned thee?"

She said, "No man, Lord." And Jesus said unto her, "Neither do I condemn thee: go, and sin no more."

Then spake Jesus again unto them, saying, "I am the light of the world: he that followeth me shall not walk in darkness, but shall have the light of life."

Luke 7:47, 50 KJV

"Wherefore I say unto thee, her sins, which are many, are forgiven; for she loved much: but to whom little is forgiven, the same loveth little."

And he said to the woman, "Thy faith hath saved thee; go in peace."

John 3:16-18 The Message

This is how much God loved the world: He gave his Son, his one and only Son. And this is why: so that no one need be destroyed; by believing in him, anyone can have a whole and lasting life. God didn't go to all the trouble of sending his Son merely to point an accusing finger, telling the world how bad it was. He came to help, to put the world right again. Anyone who trusts in him is acquitted; anyone who refuses to trust him has long since been under the death sentence without knowing it. And why? Because of that person's failure to believe in the one-of-a-kind Son of God when introduced to him.

Romans 8:1 KJV

There is therefore now no condemnation to them which are in Christ Jesus, who walk not after the flesh, but after the Spirit.

John 5:24 KJV

Verily, verily, I say unto you, He that heareth my word, and believeth on him that sent me, hath everlasting life, and shall not come into condemnation; but is passed from death unto life.

For reflection, see page 98.

To See His Face

IV
His Lap

Peeking around the pillar, I see him — that most handsome father of mine. Surrounded by constituents and members of parliament, he sits so tall and poised, listening intently to every word — whether it actually makes any sense or not. His deep voice melts through the crowd, gently yet firmly, as he responds to each and every concern.

Suddenly his white head turns in my direction. He locks my gaze, then raises one eyebrow just a hair.

I clasp my hands together, outstretched, pleading for an audience. He smiles ever so gently and waves me forward with his beautiful hands.

Some days I skip toward him, smiling and giggling softly. He winks at me and stands up to catch me in a bear hug. We snuggle for a moment; then I'm off to the rest of my day, knowing I am loved unconditionally by the High King himself.

Other times I enter the room as his princess, greeting the people with graceful nods, kissing my father on his cheek while whispering "I love you" in his ear. He rises, motioning for a moment's grace from his duties; then hugs me, kisses my forehead, and smiles into my eyes as if I am the only person in the world that matters to him.

Today, however, I plunge down the red carpet of the throne room, stumbling at his feet, throwing my head in his lap. His big, well-worn hand immediately comes to caress my cheek as my soundless tears start to flow. In a moment, he amazingly continues to listen and speak to the others nearby, handling all his affairs, yet he never forgets me. He allows me all the time I need to be with him. I absorb his life-giving energy and love through every cell of my flesh in contact with him. Even the air about him breathes peace and comfort. My tears gradually subside as my world's priorities are set right by his presence.

He senses my readiness to talk with him and requests a recess. The bystanders are directed to tables laden with a luxurious buffet.

My father's head bends over me, kissing me again and again on my hair. "My daughter, I love you so much," he breathes. "You *do* believe that, don't you? Yes, and I am so glad." He lifts my head to look into my eyes. He holds my face between his warm hands, strokes my cheek with one finger. "Are you ready to face the day again or do you need more time here?" he asks softly.

I return his gaze. A smile creeps to the corners of my mouth. "Thank you, Daddy," I whisper. "You are the best! I just needed to remind myself of the truth of who you are. And the truth of whom I am to you. Will you please send your wisdom and presence with me, as you always do?"

"Always, my child. Remember I promised — a very long

time ago."

"Yes, Daddy, and you have never broken a promise yet."

He nods at me, then squeezes me oh so tight. As he gently releases me, I turn and glide slowly toward the doors, glancing back over and over as I soak in more of his love and confidence in me.

Somehow the sun is shining brighter now. The sky is bluer. There's a tulip opening up over there. Do you see it?

Matthew 28:18-20 NKJV

And Jesus came and spoke to them, saying, "All authority has been given to Me in heaven and on earth. Go therefore and make disciples of all the nations, baptizing them in the name of the Father and of the Son and of the Holy Spirit, teaching them to observe all things that I have commanded you; and lo, I am with you always, even to the end of the age." Amen.

Colossians 1:9-12 NKJV

For this reason we also, since the day we heard it, do not cease to pray for you, and to ask that you may be filled with the knowledge of His will in all wisdom and spiritual understanding; that you may walk worthy of the Lord, fully pleasing Him, being fruitful in every good work and increasing in the knowledge of God; strengthened with all might, according to His glorious power, for all patience and longsuffering with joy; giving thanks to the Father who has qualified us to be partakers of the inheritance of the saints in the light.

For reflection, see page 100.

V
His Voice

Alarm buzzing.

　　Toilet flushing.

　　　　Radio music.

　　　　　　Shower hissing.

　　　　　　　　Kettle boiling.

　　　　　　　　　　Fridge closing.

　　　　　　　　　　　　The news.

Voices talking.

　　Feet running.

　　　　Doors slamming.

　　　　　　Motor purring.

　　　　　　　　Brakes squealing.

　　　　　　　　　　Traffic reports.

　　　　　　　　　　　　Doors slamming … again.

Constant bombarding noise.

　　Crazy busy.

Phones ringing.

Computers beeping.

Printers whirring.

Elevator Muzak.

Registers scanning.

Carts crashing.

Lunch rush.

Wipers swishing.

Politics screaming.

Traffic reports.

Pans sizzling.

Friendships calling.

Milk spilling.

Dishwasher cycling.

The news … again.

Endless harassing din.

Crazy exhausted.

Sit down.

Breathe.

Be quiet.

Emptiness of heart.

What's missing?

Gasp and sigh.

I know.

Silence.

Fidgeting.

More silence.

Choking heart's cry.

Breeze of love.

Blanket of peace.

Voice of comfort.

Quiet listening.

It's You.

Deuteronomy 28:1-6 The Message

If you listen obediently to the Voice of GOD, your God, and heartily obey all his commandments that I command you today, GOD, your God, will place you on high, high above all the nations of the world. All these blessings will come down on you and spread out beyond you because you have responded to the Voice of GOD, your God:

GOD's blessing inside the city,

GOD's blessing in the country;

GOD's blessing on your children,

the crops of your land,

the young of your livestock,

the calves of your herds,

the lambs of your flocks.

GOD's blessing on your basket and bread bowl;

GOD's blessing in your coming in,

GOD's blessing in your going out.

John 10:1-5, 27-30 NKJV

"Most assuredly, I say to you, he who does not enter the sheepfold by the door, but climbs up some other way, the same is a thief and a robber. But he who enters by the door is the shepherd of the sheep. To him the doorkeeper opens, and the sheep hear his voice; and he calls his own sheep by name and leads them out. And when he brings out his own sheep, he goes before them; and the sheep follow him, for they know his voice. Yet they will by no means follow a stranger, but will flee from him, for they do not know the voice of strangers."

"My sheep hear My voice, and I know them, and they follow Me. And I give them eternal life, and they shall never perish; neither shall anyone snatch them out of My hand. My Father, who has given them to Me, is greater than all; and no one is able to snatch them out of My Father's hand. I and My Father are one."

For reflection, see page 102.

To See His Face

VI
His Arms

Running … running … running. Got to get away … get far away so it will all leave me alone. I need space. I need quiet. I need isolation.

Dropping in the dewy green grass under the big willow tree, I curl in a ball. My eyes squeeze shut. My head pounds with pressures. Voices, demands, noise, a sense of impending doom — all wash through my brain in the wake of utter hopelessness.

Where is my promised "fulfillment"? What is this thing called "abundant life"? Why, instead, do I feel so abandoned and fearful?

A slight rustle. A warm touch on my arm. A sigh of relief. It's him.

He saw me running. He followed me to where I was.

I squint open my eyes. His hand lifts my cheek. His arms pull me close to Him.

Oh, the strength in those muscles. Firm, yet immensely gentle. He holds me, bonding me to his chest. His presence envelopes every part of me. A comforter of love warms me to the depths of my being.

I snuggle in. His chin rests on the top of my head. He kisses my hair. Rocks me softly, gently, to the rhythm of his heartbeat.

No words. No need for explanations. No expectations of me. Just the desire to be close, intimate.

Minutes pass. I don't know how many. I don't care.

I don't need separation — I need connection. I don't need emptiness — I need the filling of his Spirit. I don't need "alone time" — I need "Daddy time."

Being with Him as He desires is true fulfillment. Living with His constant touch is abundant life. Knowing He is anywhere I am every moment of every day is togetherness. Trusting in His love eliminates all my fear.

I think I need to move. I need to go back to that world I left. I hear the voices again, calling me to the next required activity of my day.

No, I can't leave the safe haven of His arms. Mentally, my brain says it's time to go. Physically, my body refuses to move. Spiritually, my soul resists. Emotionally, I'm too exhausted to face another minute out there.

Then I realize I'm moving — no, *we're* moving. He is carrying me in His arms back to the house. He knows how inadequate I am on my own, and He doesn't want me to do things that way. I hang my arms around His neck. I smile up at Him. His eyes laugh back at me with their familiar twinkle.

We're in this together. What an amazing future!

Deuteronomy 33:27a KJV

The eternal God is thy refuge, and underneath are the everlasting arms.

Mark 10:13-16 NASB

And they were bringing children to Him so that He might touch them; but the disciples rebuked them.

But when Jesus saw this, He was indignant and said to them, "Permit the children to come to Me; do not hinder them; for the kingdom of God belongs to such as these. Truly I say to you, whoever does not receive the kingdom of God like a child will not enter it at all."

And He took them in His arms and began blessing them, laying His hands on them.

For reflection, see page 104.

To See His Face

VII
His Eyes

What color are Your eyes?

At times I see them gray. Focused on the far horizons. Mirroring high stormy waters surrounding my life. At first glance, they seem cold, but then I realize they are not. They are warm steel — pure, refined, hardened with resolve, strong.

Following Your gaze, I see fog, dense fog over troubled waters. I am engulfed by fear. Fear of the unknown, unseen, uncharted waters ahead. So often I am in this place, wishing desperately for a bigger boat, a spotlight shining on the ocean, a place to anchor. What are You looking at beyond the storm clouds?

Then, through the sheets of rain, I see a path opening. A space where the wind is manageable. Actually, it's blowing my ship into the gap. Your eyes guide me into the sunlight just ahead. All I must do is look steadily into Your face and watch Your eyes to be sure of my next direction.

Yes, Your eyes are clear, strong gray for me to depend on.

Look again ... they are blue! Oh, that piercing, laser-beam blue seeing deep into my soul. They bare all before them. I cringe, knowing I have not confessed all. There are still a few messy piles in the corners of my heart which I have been unwilling to sweep up and throw away.

Your eyes find these piles immediately. Then You look at me. The blue still cuts to the depth of my being, but now I see the pain in them. You are so sad, sorrowful for my shallow little soul unable to allow You to take care of the cleaning for me. You are waiting to vacuum, to eliminate every vestige of sin, every cobweb of clinging pasts. All I must do is nod the go-ahead.

Yes, Your eyes are healing, cleansing blue for me to surrender to.

Green. You overwhelm me with Your intense green stare. Your eyes devour me with desire. They tell me they have never seen anyone as beautiful as I am. They long to watch me all day, every day, every moment, for all time. You can't get enough of my face or gestures or voice or laugh. I am Your beloved, Your princess, Your lover, Your bride.

I love the sensations running through me, yet I am frightened by them. I have never experienced such passion here on earth. No one has ever craved my presence as You do. If I don't think, my response is wild abandon.

I look again into Your hungry green depths.

All I must do is let You love me as much as You do. Can I receive this adoration without hesitation or excuses?

Yes, Your eyes are passionate, yearning green for me to

respond to with all my heart, soul and mind.

Inviting, comforting brown.   Your eyes are brown. Enveloping me with love. Pulling me to Yourself. Opening my soul to new wonders and delights as I know You more and more.

No one expresses love as You do. You lavish Your love on me, hoping I will respond with a fraction of the intensity of Your emotion. Your love never ends. It never changes. It never leaves me. It always looks and finds the best in life for me. It accepts everything about me. It believes in me no matter when everyday evidence seem to prove otherwise.

All I must do is accept Your love, respond with my heart, enjoy Your closeness, and bask in Your complete security.

Yes, Your eyes are a brown cocoon, giving me a home and safety no matter where I am.

Thank you for gazing at me with the windows to Your soul … and mine.

Psalm 33:18 NIV

But the eyes of the LORD are on those who fear him, on those whose hope is in his unfailing love.

Song of Solomon 7:10 NASB

I am my beloved's, and his desire is for me.

Psalm 32:8 KJV

I will instruct thee and teach thee in the way which thou shalt go: I will guide thee with mine eye.

For reflection, see page 106.

VIII
His Hands

Another day of ...

WIPING ...

small faces, long countertops, streaky mirrors, rivers of tears.

WASHING ...

stacks of dishes, muddy clothes, tired bodies.

MENDING ...

a leaky roof, torn jeans, stuffed animals, broken hearts.

SWEEPING ...

runaway leaves, table crumbs, dirt from under a carpet,

cobwebs from a brain.

DRESSING ...

a naked bird, naked windows, naked bodies, naked souls.

DRIVING ...

to church, to events, to the grocery store, to a place of renewal.

TOUCHING …

a cheek with a finger caress, lips to a forehead, lifting a head.

HOLDING …

clasped hands, tight shoulders, sobbing bodies, fragmented

emotions.

Raw, cracked, calloused, wrinkled hands,

abused by everyday life,

exhausted by incessant demands.

Look at the mess they have become!

Who will hold these hands of mine?

What is that? There in the center of each palm?

A terrible mark, a faded unmistakable scar, hands worn like mine,

a silhouette but deeper.

Whose hands are these?

My Father's hands.

Matthew 25:34-40 NASB

"Then the King will say to those on His right, 'Come, you who are blessed of My Father, inherit the kingdom prepared for you from the foundation of the world.

'For I was hungry, and you gave Me something to eat; I was thirsty, and you gave Me something to drink; I was a stranger, and you invited Me in; naked, and you clothed Me; I was sick, and you visited Me; I was in prison, and you came to Me.'

"Then the righteous will answer Him, 'Lord, when did we see You hungry, and feed You, or thirsty, and give You something to drink?

'And when did we see You a stranger, and invite You in, or naked, and clothe You?

'When did we see You sick, or in prison, and come to You?'

"The King will answer and say to them, 'Truly I say to you, to the extent that you did it to one of these brothers of Mine, even the least of them, you did it to Me.' "

John 20:27-29 NKJV

Then He said to Thomas, "Reach your finger here, and look at My hands; and reach your hand here, and put it into My side. Do not be unbelieving, but believing."

And Thomas answered and said to Him, "My Lord and my God!"

Jesus said to him, "Thomas, because you have seen Me, you have believed. Blessed are those who have not seen and yet have believed."

For reflection, see page 108.

IX
His House —
The Rebuilding

Another day at the jobsite. Another day of work ahead of me. Another day of wishing for some accomplishment, some sense of the end being near enough to see the proverbial light at the end of the tunnel.

He always beats me here. It's like he never leaves, just keeps working, even through the long, cold nights.

"Good morning, Daddy!" I greet him. "I need to talk with You today."

He crosses to a couple of five gallon buckets in the middle of the kitchen area, turns them over and parks on one.

"Come and sit by me, Daughter," he pats the improvised chair next to him. I obey, but I keep looking at the plywood floor. Why did I start this conversation? My words seem harsh before I even say them.

"Out with it," he laughs gently.

I'm still silent, struggling for the right way to state my unbelief. He waits a moment, then softly turns my chin and lifts my eyes to his. "I want to hear whatever you have to say, my Darling. I can see your heart and know your thoughts, but I want to hear your voice tell me what's wrong so we can solve it together."

As he looks deep into my eyes, I see his love for me and the truth of his words. He doesn't care how I say what I say – he just wants to hear me say it so we're completely honest with each other.

My tongue can't keep up as the words finally spill out. "You're here working next to me every single day. You work so hard and I do too, but it seems like we're spinning our wheels. Sure, the frame of the house is up. I can see the stunning roof lines, the huge window holes which will let in so much sunshine, and the gorgeous winding stairs. But it's been *years* and there's nothing functional in this house. The wind blows through the studs, the leaves collect inside on the floor. We're starting on the siding, but the house still feels so exposed to external forces. There's no way to warm the house or see inside at night. I'm tired of using the porta-potty to get rid of waste. No one wants to visit anymore because it's just stagnant and bare and never-changing. I'm having a hard time envisioning anything of that amazing home you and I started out to build at the beginning. Was that just a dream? Will it ever become true? I don't think I can do this anymore!"

Silent tears course down my cheeks as I choke out the last. I feel like a traitor, yet there is a strange sense of peace in my soul after my true confessions.

My daddy's eyes never leave my face. They are steady, caring, thoughtful … and then I see a glint of tears. He scoots His bucket over to me and pulls me to his chest. Love, understanding, safety, comfort, and belonging embrace me.

His chest heaves. He sniffs as his hand wipes his eyes. Then he whispers in my ear, "I'm sorry it takes so long, but I am the master craftsman and I can't rush the process, Sweetheart. You are worth too much to me to build something less than perfect for you. I feel every depth of your pain and frustration. Please continue to trust me. Building a home always brings times when it feels as if nothing is happening. I have been here so many times before with your brothers and sisters. Keep telling me how you feel, but keep believing in our dream. Can I remind you of it?"

And then, without waiting for my answer, his strong voice begins to describe once more his plans for my home. Good plans, complete plans, beautiful, peaceful, hospitable, wise plans. Somehow I realize the structure of my home is much less important than the spirit inside it. His spirit permeating every corner, creating a place no one — especially me — will want to leave. As he continues drawing colors in my mind, I see pieces of my home, completed and wonderfully functional. The edges are fuzzy and I don't know when it will be reality, but hope and belief is restored in my soul. I am just about ready to start work again for this day.

Suddenly I know this "dream" is real, right now, because He says it is. My father's sense of time is so different from mine. It's not chronological, but all-encompassing. Right now is the same as thousands of years ago or tens of years in the future. He sees my home finished today. I need to see through his eyes that it *is* finished — today. The rest of the work is just embellishments.

We sit in silence for a few minutes. I hear a single bird chirping to its mate outside in the yard. Shadows dance through the windows on the floor. A breeze picks up sawdust and sprinkles it across the floor.

"Daddy, I've got to run an errand real quick. I'll be back in a few minutes. We're going to have a picnic lunch here today and I'm inviting my favorite sisters to join me in our home."

His smile engulfs me with joy. "That's the best idea I've heard all morning! I'll be here waiting for the party!"

I've got to get busy celebrating. I need my sisters here. Hey, are you available? I want you all at my home today for a party with our Daddy.

And then we can do it again tomorrow at your home, no matter what stage it's in. OK?

Psalm 127:1a KJV

Except the LORD build the house, they labour in vain that build it.

II Corinthians 5:1-5 NIV

Now we know that if the earthly tent we live in is destroyed, we have a building from God, an eternal house in heaven, not built by human hands. Meanwhile we groan, longing to be clothed with our heavenly dwelling, because when we are clothed, we will not be found naked. For while we are in this tent, we groan and are burdened, because we do not wish to be unclothed but to be clothed with our heavenly dwelling, so that what is mortal may be swallowed up by life. Now it is God who has made us for this very purpose and has given us the Spirit as a deposit, guaranteeing what is to come.

For reflection, see page 110.

To See His Face

X
His Desire

"There you are! I've been looking all over for you." He smiles, that Daddy of mine, so strong, so special, so self-sufficient, so capable.

"Of course, I'm here," I giggle. "Did you think I ran away?"

"I sure hope not!" He laughs and grabs me in a great bear hug.

As I squeeze him back, He breathes in my ear. "I love you, Daughter."

"I love You, too, Daddy," I respond.

I sense a slight change in Him. He pulls me back to look into my face.

"Do you really love me, my child?" He asks.

I am surprised. "Yes, Daddy, You know I do."

His eyes pierce my soul. "Do you love me, my daughter?" He asks again so softly, yet so intensely.

I am confused and suddenly defensive. "Of course I do. You know that, just like You know everything. Why all the questions?"

Is this how Peter felt being questioned after denying Him? Eagerly loving Him with all his heart, hoping desperately it would be accepted — that it would be enough?

He sighs. His head bows sadly as His gaze drops.

I realize He is asking for a deeper answer from me. I breathe slowly in and out, searching for the words to adequately express the depths of my heart.

With a blinding flash of insight, I understand His question. My Daddy loves me so much and has done so much for me. And, yes, He wants me to love Him for all of that. But, most of all, He just wants me to love Him for Him … as a little girl will love her daddy just because he is her daddy. No strings attached. No expectations. Just pure, thankful, happy, playful love.

My hands gently lift His face so our eyes meet. What a familiar scene, yet *He* is usually the one lifting *my* head. I look deeply into His veiled eyes.

"Daddy, I do love You. I love You so very, very much. I love You just because. I love You in our happy moments together. I love You in spite of the painful times. I'll love You always. Do You get it? I love You … I love You … I love You! I just plain totally love You!"

My laughter is squeezed into a squeal, as my hug around His shoulders becomes a bare touch compared to His enveloping of me. As His arms relax just a little, I laugh.

"Hey, Daddy, You know what?"

"What, Baby Doll?" He grins back.

"I love You!"

"And I love you MORE!"

I am amazed as I realize the High King of Heaven *wants* my love, *craves* my love, *desires* my love. I guess He did create me just for that reason … to be with Him as His daughter forever.

Deuteronomy 30:19b-20a NKJV

Therefore choose life, that both you and your descendants may live; that you may love the LORD your God, that you may obey His voice, and that you may cling to Him, for He is your life and the length of your days.

I John 4:18-19 NKJV

There is no fear in love; but perfect love casts out fear, because fear involves torment. But he who fears has not been made perfect in love. We love Him because He first loved us.

For reflection, see page 112.

XI
His Answer

Tears course down my cheeks. My hands pound the steering wheel. I know I should pull over before I crash the car, but I just keep driving … like the driving tidal wave of emotions overwhelming me.

"Why? Why?" I scream, wishing I had more words to describe my agony. "Why me, Father? Why did you give me this incredibly huge burden to bear? I can't do this! I can't do this!"

Stopping at a light allows me a moment to collect my thoughts. Now my words come ....

"This thing is too much for me to handle. It takes me beyond my limits every single day, many times a day. I feel like I'm completely incompetent, always frustrated, a walking bundle of anger exploding at the least spark. It drains my creative energy, squelches my hope, keeps my insides in constant turmoil – and there is no end in sight! How can you love me and yet leave me with this heavy load? It's not fair! You must take it away! I ask you to take it from me now! Do you hear me? Now!"

Silence. I cruise down the entrance ramp to the freeway and speed up to match the cars next to me. There's nothing in the air, in my mind, in my soul.

"You can't hide from me, Daddy!" I pout out loud. "I know

you're out there and you said you hear me so how about an answer? I need an answer! Now!"

Again silence. I huff and puff. I conjure up my heated emotions again.

"So tell me why and I'll shut up about this. I just need a reason so I can understand and make a plan to work with it and solve it and get beyond it. I need a solution – a light at the end of the tunnel, so to speak. Just tell me why, Father. Just tell me why so I can ..."

His finger touches my lips to stop the torrent of words. I freeze. He was always here — I just wasn't willing to feel or hear him.

My heart listens. My mouth shuts. And I wait for him to speak.

"Daughter, even if I told you why, you wouldn't understand the reason. You live in a finite world, limited by absolutes which insure your physical safety and reality. My existence has no limits, no confining edges. My time encompasses all of eternity at once. My mind creates, destroys, changes and stabilizes all at the same time. I know everything about you — from the moment you were conceived, to the moment right now, to the many moments in your future, and our eternity together. I designed your life on earth to maximize your potential and achieve my great purposes for you. No masterpiece is created without struggle and massive effort. You are my masterpiece, my precious daughter. I want you perfect,

62

beautiful, and shining with glory. So, trust me. Listen for me. Trust me, now and forever. Just keep trusting me every minute of every day. I do know what I'm doing. I do know the future of your story. It does have a happy ending, Princess! Just trust me."

I know he's waiting for my answer now. I drive a while, contemplating what he asks of me. Can I trust him? Do I trust him? Trust. What a multitude of nuances and connotations come with one little word!

No one in my world has ever been truly trustworthy. Everyone has let me down in some little way ... or big way. They promise something and forget. They start strong with you and then lose steam before the end. The anniversary or birthday passes without recognition. Careless words are spoken that cut deeply.

Would it be different with my Father?

He created me — for a purpose. He loves me enough to sacrifice his only son to die a criminal's death and be separated from him — the only time in eternity past or future — long enough to conquer the devil in his domain. He's building a mansion for me in heaven where I will live forever, seeing him every day, touching his hand, hearing his voice, giving and receiving hugs from him.

Come to think of it, what is this life on earth? Just a little time to learn about him, accept his gift of salvation, and start the process of becoming perfect once more — as he had designed mankind in the Garden of Eden. And he is with me constantly. He doesn't expect me to do this life alone. He doesn't *want* me to do it alone!

He promises everything I need if I just ask him. So, can I accept that he has just given me all the answer I need?

It's my exit. I veer right, down the off ramp, and into a parking lot. I stop driving. I stop fighting. I stop thinking rationally. I've gotten in the way of his purpose for me.

"Yes, Daddy, I'll trust you — but you've got to give me the ability to trust you every moment of every day. My limited mind and body aren't going to do it — I know you know that! So, yes, I'll trust you as you help me trust you."

I know he's smiling – that wonderful, chuckling smile at the corners of his mouth when he's delighting in me, so glad to share life with me, so proud of me as his daughter, and so ready to be my Father in every way.

I know life isn't going to be easier today. The emotions of anger, frustration, and incompetence will still arise and start to overwhelm me, but I can say, "Help, Daddy, help me trust you," over and over again if I need to. I bet he can't wait to hear me say it — over and over again.

II Samuel 22: 1-4, 31-33 NKJV

Then David spoke to the LORD the words of this song, on
the day when the LORD had delivered him from the hand of all his
enemies, and from the hand of Saul. And he said:

"The LORD is my rock and my fortress and my deliverer;

The God of my strength, in whom I will trust;

My shield and the horn of my salvation,

My stronghold and my refuge;

My Savior, You save me from violence.

I will call upon the LORD, who is worthy to be praised;

So shall I be saved from my enemies.

As for God, His way is perfect;

The word of the LORD is proven;

He is a shield to all who trust in Him.

For who is God, except the LORD?

And who is a rock, except our God?

God is my strength and power,

And He makes my way perfect."

Psalm 20:4-9 NKJV

> May He grant you according to your heart's desire,
>> And fulfill all your purpose.
> We will rejoice in your salvation,
>> And in the name of our God we will set up our banners!
>> May the LORD fulfill all your petitions.
> Now I know that the LORD saves His anointed;
>> He will answer him from His holy heaven
>> With the saving strength of His right hand.
> Some trust in chariots, and some in horses;
>> But we will remember the name of the LORD our God.
> They have bowed down and fallen;
>> But we have risen and stand upright.
> Save, LORD!
>> May the King answer us when we call.

For reflection, see page 114.

XII
His Peace

So elusive.

Why can't I find it?

That "peace which surpasses all understanding"

which "will guard my heart and mind

through Christ Jesus"?

I've asked for it, Father.

I've looked for it.

I keep waiting for it.

But it's not here.

What must I do to gain this prize?

What else do You want me to do?

Instead another life tornado comes silently down,

twisting its finger of fear

into my carefully balanced existence,

wreaking utter havoc to what "should have been."

Too many of these have come too quickly.

This time I cannot pretend anymore.

Stresses have me on the rack.

Functioning thought is obsolete.

Physical strength has evaporated.

My lips whisper, "Help me, please, Daddy!"

It's all I can muster.

I don't even know what I'm asking for.

I am dangling by a glistening thread of a spider's web above

a pitch black abyss.

But He is here.

His hand is under my feet.

His arms bear me gently to firm ground.

That in itself is amazing.

But, more so, my heart and mind …

He is guarding them — with His peace.

An indescribable calm,

washing through me,

assuring me of protection, hope and a bright future.

I am permeated by His peace
— and it stays and stays and stays.

There is no explanation why.
The tornado's strength increases.
It howls around me,
threatening to shatter my life as I know it!

But I am still at peace.
It is well with my soul.
His peace by His grace in His timing.

When I quit trying,
He gave His matchless gift to His beloved … me.

John 14:26–27 NKJV

But the Helper, the Holy Spirit, whom the Father will send in My name, He will teach you all things, and bring to your remembrance all things that I said to you. Peace I leave with you, My peace I give to you; not as the world gives do I give to you. Let not your heart be troubled, neither let it be afraid.

John 16:33 NKJV

These things I have spoken to you, that in Me you may have peace. In the world you will have tribulation; but be of good cheer, I have overcome the world.

Philippians 4:6-7 NKJV

Be anxious for nothing, but in everything by prayer and supplication, with thanksgiving, let your requests be made known to God; and the peace of God, which surpasses all understanding, will guard your hearts and minds through Christ Jesus.

For reflection, see page 116.

XIII
His Design

No more running. I am caught. Your hand grasps my spirit tightly. I can barely breathe. Yet I still struggle, flailing my well-worn excuses against Your silken bonds.

It's taken a while to get here. At first, You gently called me, encouraged me, waited for me to drift Your way. When I continued in my oblivious routine, You dropped a few obstacles into my path, shaking up my carefully controlled existence.

But I was stubborn, turning my body toward You — not my eyes or my heart.

Yet You worked with my half-hearted willingness. You used circumstances and events to touch my soul. You never stopped pursuing me, never for a moment believed I would not become who You designed me to be.

And now, in these last weeks, You have clearly shown me what it is You created me to do in Your kingdom. This position can only be filled by me. It is so specific!

If I do not do this, it will never be done.

And then there will be a gaping hole in the intricate tapestry of Your world, a critical missing piece in the complex puzzle of life, a colorless void shaped exactly like my gifts.

I am terrified. Your hand moves to show me Your plan. It is

impossible! No way can I pull this off! I don't even know how to start!

You turn me so I must see Your face. Your gaze captures mine. The heartbeat in Your fingers mirrors my pulse. You pat Your lap. I hesitantly sit down. Your arms engulf me.

My head drops to Your shoulder of its own volition. My muscles collapse, signaling my stubborn will to do the same. Tears wet my eyes, then slowly wet my cheeks and fall to Your shoulder.

Can I actually do this thing You are calling me to do?

"Yes!" You answer my thoughts. "I already have everything poised in time and space to appear when you need it. I don't play the odds, Baby Girl. I AM. All you need is faith — and I've got more than enough for you.

"I'm not asking you to force, coerce, or strong-arm anything to happen. I'm just asking you to be you. The you I created with special talents specific to this path. I will walk next to you — every moment side by side, hand in hand, heart to heart.

"Please come. I know it's a little rough right now, but I love you too much to allow you to miss the ultimate opportunity of being all you were made to be. It's *way* better than Disneyland ... trust me!"

How can my Daddy so easily dissipate all my fears? All my inadequacies? All my questions? But You do. So quickly, so smoothly, so completely.

My mind tells me to be rational and keep protesting. My

heart races with anticipation toward the possibilities You extend.

"OK," I speak aloud. "Let's do this!"

Your smile takes my breath away. I had no idea how much You cared about my part in Your kingdom, in this adventure You planned for us.

"I love you, Daughter. This is going to be really good …!"

II Timothy 1:8-10 The Message

So don't be embarrassed to speak up for our Master or for me, his prisoner. Take your share of suffering for the Message along with the rest of us. We can only keep on going, after all, by the power of God, who first saved us and then called us to this holy work. We had nothing to do with it. It was all his idea, a gift prepared for us in Jesus long before we knew anything about it. But we know it now. Since the appearance of our Savior, nothing could be plainer: death defeated, life vindicated in a steady blaze of light, all through the work of Jesus.

Ephesians 1:15-19 The Message

That's why, when I heard of the solid trust you have in the Master Jesus and your outpouring of love to all the followers of Jesus, I couldn't stop thanking God for you — every time I prayed, I'd think of you and give thanks. But I do more than thank. I ask — ask the God of our Master, Jesus Christ, the God of glory — to make you intelligent and discerning in knowing him personally, your eyes focused and clear, so that you can see exactly what it is he is calling you to do, grasp the immensity of this glorious way of life he has for his followers, oh, the utter extravagance of his work in us who trust him — endless energy, boundless strength!

For reflection, see page 118.

XIV
His Calling

I want to do something important. I want to contribute in a way that makes a difference. I want someone to miss my presence when my life here on earth is finished.

All those statements are true. And, yet, there is a desire much deeper within me. An impassioned quest more immense than mere words can express.

Significance. I want to be significant to someone. Sought after. Admired. Heard. Desired. Enfolded. Treasured. Delighted in. Trusted. Truly loved.

My days are spent searching for this thing that drives me. I look for it from everyone I meet, hoping someday it will be there and my mission will be completed so I can rest.

But I can't find it. I don't feel it. My mind is frenzied. My heart is breaking. My soul is suffocating. Why is it so hard to find someone who really cares about me?

Yes, I know my mother loves me — at least she says she does. But I don't believe it deep down.

And my father? He's the first person I wished so much would satisfy this longing in me. But he's never said much of anything; I guess he's tried to show me he cares. It all just falls very short of what I need.

Then there are all the boys I've known. Always a good friend, a great buddy, but never anything more important. Forgotten when the next pretty face walks through the door.

And the men? A revolving door of opportunities to serve, make them look good, satisfy their need for conquest. Nothing for me.

My hope fades. My spirit is crushed. My life flame flickers in the atmosphere of lack around me. Will I never find fulfillment?

Abruptly I open my soul's blinded eyes. I have been in pursuit when He's simply waiting for me to stop running.

I lay my head in His lap.

He loves me with an everlasting love. From before the foundations of the earth He has known me intimately. He planned every one of my days and can't wait to share them with me. He never slumbers or sleeps. He will not let anyone snatch me out of His protecting hand. His plans for me are greater than I can imagine. He has given me talents beyond what I have had the courage to discover on my own. He pursues me, yet waits for me to turn to Him. He is so gentle; He never pushes me to respond to Him. And yet He desires me above anything else. He chooses to be with me, talk with me, listen to me, share every moment of life with me.

He is my Father. My best friend. The lover of my soul.

I am His daughter, a princess. I am His friend and

76

confidant. I am His bride adorned with jewels.

I have found what I am looking for.

I am significant to Him. He created me because He knew there was no one else who could be who I am and do what I do.

He knew the world needed me.

And I need Him. To still my restless heart. To fill my soul's longings. To satisfy the void deep inside me.

I am sought after. Admired. Heard. Desired. Enfolded. Treasured. Delighted in. Trusted. Truly loved. I am significant.

Ephesians 4:4-7 The Message

You were all called to travel on the same road and in the same direction, so stay together, both outwardly and inwardly. You have one Master, one faith, one baptism, one God and Father of all, who rules over all, works through all, and is present in all. Everything you are and think and do is permeated with Oneness.

But that doesn't mean you should all look and speak and act the same. Out of the generosity of Christ, each of us is given his own gift.

I Corinthians 12:14-18 The Message

I want you to think about how all this makes you more significant, not less. A body isn't just a single part blown up into something huge. It's all the different-but-similar parts arranged and functioning together. If Foot said, "I'm not elegant like Hand, embellished with rings; I guess I don't belong to this body," would that make it so? If Ear said, "I'm not beautiful like Eye, limpid and expressive; I don't deserve a place on the head," would you want to remove it from the body? If the body was all eye, how could it hear? If all ear, how could it smell? As it is, we see that God has carefully placed each part of the body right where he wanted it.

For reflection, see page 120.

XV
His Beloved

"I'm engaged ... still!" I stretch, soaking in the joy and anticipation of my thoughts. Birds' songs are sweet outside my window. Sunshine creeps into every corner of my body. A smile spreads across my mouth.

A brand new era of my life started the day I met him. I am no longer an "I," but a "we." Together he and I face the minutes, hours, days, and years of life. Together we will conquer fears, banish doubts, develop talents, grow in love and grace. Our future is truly bright!

My mind remembers special moments we have shared. Like the first time I met his eyes and was inextricably pulled into its depths. I was finally home. I could barely tear myself away from him to respond to others around me. Yet I followed his lead, and found myself in a kind of a dance, gliding smoothly from interaction to interaction with him, living fully each moment of the night.

Or the day tragedy hit. I was devastated, incoherent, inconsolable. His strong arms simply held me until my sobs quieted and my breath returned. Then with gentle fingers, he raised my face to his, kissed me, and listened without a word as I poured it all out before him. In his presence, clarity and strength were renewed. I was able to pick up the pieces of my life with him by my side, my companion and friend.

Or our afternoon spent at the park. We relaxed on the grass, shared the beauty of the blossoming trees, ate a picnic lunch, took a nap in the shade, then rolled down a hill and played tag like children. We walked hand in hand much of that day, our souls connecting without words.

He calls me "Beloved." That is like "my darling," "I adore you," "sweetheart," and "my desire" all rolled into one. It takes my breath away every time I hear his voice call my name. I still can't believe he wants me — *every* part of me — to be with him all the moments of my life, forever. Never apart, no matter what.

Not to say absolutely every minute with him is entirely painless. There have been those times he was *so* right and I was *so* wrong — and I had to admit it … out loud. Or when I twisted the truth a little and his eyes caught me covering up. And — more than once — when I just messed everything up and needed forgiveness for a multitude of stupid actions.

But he always wipes the slate clean and encourages me. He truly believes in me … my good intentions, my gifts and talents, my heart's calling. He knows I am more than my mistakes.

He is so much more than I ever imagined in a husband. Everything I dreamed of plus all the things I never knew I needed and wanted. He is my soul mate.

I've heard being married is a choice made by each partner

every single day.

The Lover of my soul has pledged His love to me every single day since I met Him. He anticipates our wedding feast in His Father's banquet hall not too far in the future. I can't wait to live with Him as He rules His Kingdom forever. But wait … He's already ruling and I'm already with Him. Isn't it glorious?

Deuteronomy 33:12b KJV

The beloved of the LORD shall dwell in safety by him; and the Lord shall cover him all the day long, and he shall dwell between his shoulders.

Jeremiah 31:3b NKJV

"Yes, I have loved you with an everlasting love;

Therefore with lovingkindness I have drawn you."

For reflection, see page 122.

XVI
His House —
The Mansion

Perfect. Absolutely pristine. Ultimate curb appeal. Is this the right address?

My key fits the lock. I step inside. Words escape me. It's too lovely to describe, beyond anything I've ever imagined.

I slip off my shoes. My feet begin to explore. Favorite colors surround me. Inviting doorways lead me smoothly from room to room. Light cascades gently over all, illuminating shadowed corners. A kaleidoscope of textures and textiles engulf my senses. My fingers run tenderly over finished surfaces, marveling at the rich handiwork.

Beauty embraces me from all sides. I could live in this place forever and never take my surroundings for granted. My spirit is lifted, inspired, catalyzed.

Do I dare sit down in this deep, downy upholstered sofa … for just a few minutes? To bask in this solace of beauty and peace?

This place is not just a physical shelter; it's a haven for body, mind, and soul.

Muscles relax.

Aches subside.

Thoughts calm.

Emotions untangle.

Plans clarify.

Priorities straighten.

Purpose solidifies.

Wisdom reigns.

Strength renews.

Accomplishment ensues.

There is something so familiar and comfortable about it all. But also new and exhilarating.

I make my way back toward the entry, wishing I could turn around and experience it all again — and again. I'm sold. I want to live here, in this house. Whatever the price, I've got to find a way!

Busy planning, I put on my shoes and reach for my phone. I think if I say the right words, explaining the uniqueness of this location, potential future value, outstanding craftsmanship … I'll get it. Oh, I want it!

Pushing the door open, I crash against an obstacle.

"It's you!" I exclaim. "I was just going to call you. How did you know to be here? You have got to see this house. It's incredible! It's perfect!"

He allows me to pull him across the threshold and down the halls as I babble incessantly. I see his eyes light up as we enter various rooms. I know he's getting as excited as I am. Yes, I will have this house for my own!

As we finish the grand tour, I turn to him. "Please, please, I want this house. I know we've been working on that other one for a long time — and, please don't take this wrong. It's wonderful and I love it. But this place is beyond words. It is perfect for me. It would make me happy forever. I would take such good care of it. I need it — desperately! Can we sell that other one and buy this one? Tell me what I have to do and I'll do it. Anything!"

Suddenly I realize what I'm asking. He has designed and built my other house tirelessly for years. I thought there could never be another home as amazing as that one. And here I am, negating all his work, telling him it wasn't worth the effort in the long run because it isn't good enough for me. For *me* ... as if I even have a right to choose after all I've screwed up in this building process.

I haven't even been helping him as much as I used to. I often use excuses to get out of stuff. I take longer than I should to get things done. Sometimes my work's not as excellent as we planned because I get tired and cut corners.

Didn't I say I'd do whatever it took to build the other house? And look at me now. Fickle, wishy-washy, fly-by-night help — that's me.

He's watching me. I'm sure my emotions are playing out over my face. I am so ashamed of my behavior. Wish I could eat my last words. Wish I could learn how to stop being stupid. Wish I

85

had better control of myself. Wish ....

"Daughter? Does this house remind you of any other home?"

His voice interrupts my dark thoughts. I hesitantly glance up at Him.

"Yes, a little, but I can't tell You where. Do You know?"

His mouth quirks at the edges. "Yes," He states.

"Wherever it is, I know I wasn't as affected by it as I am with this place," I respond, hoping He'll elaborate a little.

"I was — and am."

Silence. I wait for Him to go on.

"What do you mean? Where is the other house? I need some help here."

He turns me around to face the house again. "Look. Really look."

My eyes work to take everything in once more. My brain is overwhelmed trying to make sense of His request. What is it that is familiar? Where have I seen all this before?

Suddenly I know. I spin around.

"This is my other house, isn't it? Only so much better because it is completely finished, and ... and ... there is something more here. Something I don't understand, but it's permanent!"

He smiles broadly.

"Now you've got it! This *is* your house, the one we've been working on together. I just transformed a few things so it fit into this neighborhood. Even though it looks finished, you can't move in quite yet. I've still got some work to do."

"Why did You let me get the key, then? I don't think I want to wait. Can't You finish it up right now and we can be done, and I can live here, now and forever?"

Shaking His head gently, He pulls me into a hug.

"I love it when you get so fired up," He laughs. "How can I make you understand? It's not time for you to live here yet. I wanted you to see this home as I see it so you would once again believe in our dream. So you would again pursue excellence in every detail. So you can look forward with great anticipation to the perfect end result — even more perfect than this glimpse. And so you can joyfully be with me as I finish the work.

"I know it's hard to wait and the building process is hard work. There is a season for everything, Darling. And every season is precious and perfect in its time."

He's building me a mansion made specifically for me. We're working on it together, and, when He's finished, I will live in it forever — with Him.

Perfect. Absolutely perfect. The right address ... for eternity.

John 14:1-6 NKJV

"Let not your heart be troubled; you believe in God, believe also in Me. In My Father's house are many mansions; if it were not so, I would have told you. I go to prepare a place for you.

"And if I go and prepare a place for you, I will come again and receive you to Myself; that where I am, there you may be also. And where I go you know, and the way you know."

Thomas said to Him, "Lord, we do not know where You are going, and how can we know the way?"

Jesus said to him, "I am the way, the truth, and the life. No one comes to the Father except through Me."

Revelation 21:4 NKJV

And God will wipe away every tear from their eyes; there shall be no more death, nor sorrow, nor crying. There shall be no more pain, for the former things have passed away.

Hebrews 11:13-16 The Message

Each one of these people of faith died not yet having in hand what was promised, but still believing. How did they do it? They saw it way off in the distance, waved their greeting, and accepted the fact that they were transients in this world. People who live this way make it plain that they are looking for their true home. If they were homesick for the old country, they could have gone back any time they wanted. But they were after a far better country than that — heaven country. You can see why God is so proud of them, and has a City waiting for them.

For reflection, see page 124.

To See His Face

As You Continue

I pray you have been blessed by Daddy through the pages of this book. He gave me these words to share with you. He caused this book to come to you. He longs for your constant companionship — 24/7.

This is a time of uncertainty for many people. There is a pervading sense of much in our world being out of control, hurtling toward a scary crisis. The only real way to fight these fears is by knowing you are His daughter and trusting Him who is sovereign, completely in control, and working everything together according to His great and mighty plan. Focusing on Him clarifies everything ... so we must encourage each other to keep doing this every moment of every day!

If you don't know Him as your Father, you can. He is separated from you by the wrong things you've done, both thoughts and actions. You know what these things are because He created you in His likeness, with a conscience that differentiates between good and evil. He came to earth to die on the cross to wipe out your sin and shame — forever. His forgiveness is a gift. You only have to believe in Him, that He is real, and accept His gift of redemption. Then you are no longer separated from Him, now and for eternity. There really are no strings attached, as once you see His face, you will always want to do what He calls you to do. And He gives you whatever you need to do it.

If you have accepted His gift of forgiveness and new life in your past, how's your house coming? Do you see His face? Feel His touch? Know His voice? I pray you do — more and more, all day, every day, as your relationship with Him grows and changes and exhilarates.

I am honored you chose to spend time with me.

With love,

Faith Gallatin

I would thoroughly enjoy hearing from you
about your experiences with our Daddy
— or your questions about Him.

Please visit

www.ToSeeHisFace.com

to share your reflections, journey with your sisters,
and discover other books in this series.

We'll be waiting for you!

For Reflection

His Invitation

ഔ *Who are <u>you</u>?*

ഔ *Do you believe His invitation is true and real?*

ഔ *What's your next "move"?*

ഔ *My thoughts:*

His House — The Burning

  &so; *Do you believe He loves you unconditionally despite what you've done?*

  &so; *Why does He ask you to listen and consider His words, rather than demand this?*

  &so; *Will you trust Him to rebuild your home? What are the costs?*

  &so; *My thoughts:*

His Forgiveness

                What comprises the struggle for control of souls? Your soul?

                How does He lift your head?

                Do you ask for and receive His forgiveness as often as you need it?

                My thoughts:

His Lap

ɞ *What does it mean to call Him "Daddy"? Can you? Do you?*

ɞ *How are your priorities set right by His presence?*

ɞ *How are you impacted by the fact that He is <u>always</u> available?*

ɞ *My thoughts:*

His Voice

ɣ *Do you recognize His voice?*

ɣ *What noises in your life block His voice from being heard?*

ɣ *How can you make sure you hear His voice first and foremost on a moment by moment basis?*

ɣ *My thoughts:*

His Arms

❧ *When have you run from someone or something?*

❧ *How does His presence dissolve your fears?*

❧ *Do you understand you don't have to do it all on your own? What does that mean to you?*

❧ *My thoughts:*

For Reflection

105

His Eyes

෨ *What does it mean to discover the colors of His eyes?*

෨ *Why is it hard to interact with and accept some of His emotions?*

෨ *Do you believe He guides, heals, yearns for, and loves you — intensely, deeply?*

෨ *My thoughts:*

His Hands

ᛋ *What do your hands look like, feel like?*

ᛋ *What do His scars mean to you?*

ᛋ *How does it feel to have His hands holding yours?*

ᛋ *My thoughts:*

His House — The Rebuilding

ଚ୬ *Why does He want to hear your concerns?*

ଚ୬ *What is it like to experience His timing?*

ଚ୬ *Do you see your dreams through His eyes? Do you invite others to share His dreams for them?*

ଚ୬ *My thoughts:*

His Desire

℥ *Do you know God longs to be loved by you?*

℥ *Do you love Him most of all? "More than these" ... all the other distractions around you?*

℥ *Do you understand you can start loving Him "more" this very moment?*

℥ *My thoughts:*

His Answer

ℛ *Why is it so important to be honest with God about your feelings?*

ℛ *How do things change when you ask for His help?*

ℛ *What does "trust" mean to you? Will you trust Him? No matter what?*

ℛ *My thoughts:*

His Peace

ಸಂ *Why is peace sometimes elusive?*

ಸಂ *What does it mean to know His hand is under your feet?*

ಸಂ *Why can you experience His peace in the midst of the storm?*

ಸಂ *My thoughts:*

His Design

ɕɔ *What does it mean to be pursued by Him?*

ɕɔ *What is the tapestry of His world?*

ɕɔ *Are you still running? Looking at Him? Crying on His lap? Saying "Let's do this!"?*

ɕɔ *My thoughts:*

His Calling

ɞ *What is it like to open your soul's blinded eyes?*

ɞ *What is it like to be in His presence?*

ɞ *Why are you significant? Be specific.*

ɞ *My thoughts:*

His Beloved

෨ *Do you know you are more than your mistakes?*

෨ *Why do clarity and strength renew in His presence?*

෨ *What is it like to follow His lead and dance with Him?*

෨ *My thoughts:*

His House -- The Mansion

  ℴ *What would it feel like to be in a place of haven for your body, mind, and soul?*

  ℴ *Why does He work so hard to renew your vision of His dreams with and for you?*

  ℴ *Do you know what your address will be for eternity? Describe it.*

  ℴ *My thoughts:*